Ten Day Health Challenge, Daniel Fast, & Morning Battle Prayer

Contents

Copyright page

Copyright Page
2023
Printed in the USA (Print Version):

Published by JEllis1 Publishing

DISCLAIMER:

THIS BOOK DOES NOT PROVIDE MEDICAL ADVICE

The information contained in this book, including, but not limited to, text, graphics, images, and other materials, is for informational purposes only. The content in this book is not intended to serve as a substitute for professional medical advice, diagnosis, or treatment. Always consult your physician or a qualified healthcare provider for any questions about a medical condition or treatment before starting a new healthcare regimen. Never ignore professional medical advice or postpone seeking it due to information read in this book.

Dedication

This book is first dedicated to the Holy Spirit, who gave me the revelation and inspiration to write it.

To my beautiful wife, Summer, my perfect soulmate, my helpmate, my best friend, my everything! I couldn't have accomplished this without your amazing support.

To my awesome children for their unwavering love and support.

To my beloved parents, the late Mr. John Ehigiator, and the awesome "Iye," Mrs. Mary Ehigiator, who molded me into the person I am today.

To my spiritual parents, the late Apostle Michael Christian, and the amazing Mama Blossom Christian, for believing in me and for their continuous prayer and support.

To my precious family and church family (NationTakers Ministries) for all their love and support.

To everyone who has influenced my life in one way or another, all of you have made this book possible.

Introduction

Welcome to the Ten-Day Health Challenge, Daniel Fast, and Morning Battle Prayer, a guide for your health and well-being. Brothers and sisters, ladies, and gentlemen, in these next ten days, I invite you to believe in God for a complete body and mind makeover, health restoration, and healing from sickness and diseases. When God placed this on my heart, I saw people delivered from their long-lasting situations: blood pressure normalized, cancer disappeared, cholesterol corrected, migraines gone, thyroid problems healed, irregular heartbeat regulated, weight loss activated, strength restored, and many experienced healings.

Our God is a good, awesome, and faithful God. When He gives us an instruction, and we follow through, we will see results. Just look at Abraham and Moses. When Abraham followed the instructions God gave him, he received results. When Moses followed the instructions God gave him, he also received results. So, when God instructs us, and we follow through, we too will see results.

As you follow through with this Ten-Day Health Challenge, Daniel Fast, and Morning Battle Prayer, I want you to understand that this is directed towards your health and well-being. The Lord desires His children to be in good health and to prosper in every ramification of their lives.

"Beloved, I pray that you may prosper in all things and be in health, just as your soul prospers." (3 John 1:2, NKJV).

You should be living a healthy lifestyle. Everything in you should be healthy. Have this mindset as you embark on this ten-day journey. This journey will mark a new beginning in your life, it will be a season for you to reset and to live in health, wellness, and wholeness.

Event Triggers Decision

It was Christmas Day in 1994 when I fell ill. This happened when I lived in Nigeria. In Nigeria, malaria and fever were common among other sicknesses. However, after that incident, I made a decision: I no longer wanted to get sick. Christmas was a grand event that we all looked forward to. It was the day we got to wear our new clothes, visit family and friends, and enjoy all kinds of delicious food. Missing out on Christmas made me especially unhappy. So, I told the Lord my decision and went into a covenant agreement with Him for divine health, and He graciously granted my request. By the grace of God, I have had divine health since December of 1994, and an event is what triggered that decision.

I want you to understand that the same God is still alive, and you can trust in Him today as you embark on this health challenge. Believe that God will give you divine health and restore your well-being. Sickness will have no room in your life. Declare that you will live a healthy and strong life. For His Word says that there was none feeble among them. This will be your portion in the mighty name of Jesus.

"…And there was none feeble among His tribes." (Psalm 105:37, NKJV).

God will strengthen everything in you. You do not have to grow old and become weak and tired. The Word of the Lord says that even in old age, His people still bear fruits.

"They shall still bear fruit in old age; They shall be fresh and flourishing" (Psalm 92:14, NKJV).

Caleb was of old age when he stated that he felt as strong as he was in his youth. These people were men and women of God, individuals who believed in the Word of God and God did wonders for them.

"As yet I am as strong this day as on the day that Moses sent me; just as my strength was then, so now is my strength for war, both for going out and for coming in." (Joshua 14:11, NKJV).

As you embark on this journey, I encourage you to wholeheartedly commit to it. The devil will challenge you, and temptations will arise. Oh yes, think of the sweet smell of cookies and donuts. Delicious food will come your way, and sometimes, that delicious food will even be offered to you for free! Temptation will urge you to indulge, but you have to say, "I have proposed in my heart that I will not defile myself with this delicacy." Just like Daniel, you have to say, "in these ten days I will not defile myself, I will stay true to it, and I will see the positive result."

If you have been struggling to lose weight, let this season be the time when you wholeheartedly commit to it and achieve your goals through this ten-day journey. When you get started, weigh yourself, record it, and track your progress over the next ten days. Trust in the Lord that every cell in your body will activate for weight loss, and that stubborn weight will vanish. If you have been struggling with headaches, believe in God that they will be gone on

7

this journey. Weight loss and headaches are just examples. I would suggest you examine your health and identify areas of concern. Whatever the issues may be, trust that as you embark on this challenge, your situation will align with the Word of God, and you will be delivered.

My prayer for you is that as you engage and commit to this ten-day challenge, God himself will heal and restore you to total wholeness, nothing missing and nothing broken. Like Daniel, you will be able to make the declaration that you are ten times better!

"But **Daniel resolved not to defile himself** with the **royal food and wine**, and he asked the chief official for permission not to **defile himself** this way. Now God had caused the official to show **favor and compassion** to Daniel, but the official told Daniel, "I am afraid of my lord the king, who has assigned your food and drink. Why should he see you looking worse than the other young men your age? The king would then have my head because of you." Daniel then said to the guard whom the chief official had appointed over Daniel, Hananiah, Mishael and Azariah, "Please test your servants for **ten days**: Give us nothing but **vegetables to eat and water to drink**. Then compare our appearance with that of the young men who eat the royal food and treat your servants in accordance with what you see."

So, he agreed to this and tested them for **ten days**. At the end of the **ten days,** they **looked healthier and better nourished** than any of the young men who ate the royal food. So, the guard took away their choice of food and the wine they were to drink and gave them vegetables instead. To these four young men God gave **knowledge and**

understanding of all kinds of literature and learning. And Daniel could **understand visions and dreams of all kinds**.

At the end of the time set by the king to bring them into his service, the chief official presented them to Nebuchadnezzar. The king talked with them, and he found nonequal to Daniel, Hananiah, Mishael and Azariah; so, they entered the king's service. In every matter of wisdom and understanding about which the king questioned them, he found them **ten times better** than all the magicians and enchanters in his whole kingdom." (Daniel 1:8-18, NKJV).

Daniel made an intentional act not to defile himself with the royal food and wine. He was determined to do something, irrespective of the temptation and the danger ahead. God granted him favor and compassion.

I pray that as you embark on this journey, you will also find favor in the sight of God and man. By the end of these ten days, you will not only look healthier, but you will also become better, well nourished, and better than your companions. For Daniel and these young men, the key was not solely the vegetables they ate and the water they drank; it was the hand of God upon them. As you participate in this challenge, remember that you are not alone, the hand and the glory of God are upon you. Therefore, if you wholeheartedly engage in this challenge and trust in God's Word, you will experience transformative results.

Make this resolution and commitment to God: <u>"O God, over the next ten days, I will discipline myself to follow the instructions given in this book!"</u>

How To Use This Book

This book serves as a practical guide to achieving breakthroughs, experiencing deliverance, and maintaining a healthy lifestyle.

Each chapter corresponds to a day and encompasses both spiritual and physical applications. The daily spiritual practice involves scripture readings from the book of Proverbs, prayer points to be recited throughout the day, declarations to be made intermittently, and a communion service to conclude the spiritual aspect of this journey in the evening. Additionally, it includes a concluding prayer for each day's sessions.

The daily physical regimen includes reminders for proper hydration (such as drinking water or a healthy substitute), making healthy meal choices, and recommendations for participating in a Daniel Fast and engaging in exercise.

Below are two lists: food to avoid and food to enjoy. These are merely examples intended to give you an idea.

Food to Avoid

I would recommend avoiding the following foods and beverages throughout the duration of this health challenge:

Added Sugar	Poultry
Artificial Sweeteners	Processed Foods
Bread (Leavened)	Preservatives
Caffeine	Refined Grains
Dairy Products	Refined Oils
Deep-fried food	Seafood
Eggs	Soda
Fish	Solid Fats
Meat	Yeast

Food to Enjoy

I would recommend enjoying the following foods during the duration of this health challenge. You can choose any of these for your Daniel Fast meals.

Apples	Eggplant	Pecans
Almonds	Garlic	Peas
Artichoke	Grape	Peanuts
Asparagus	Hazelnuts	Peppers
Avocado	Herbs	Pistachios
Banana	Kiwi	Plums
Blueberries	Lemon	Pineapple
Blackberries	Lettuce	Pumpkin
Broccoli	Lentils	Seeds
Beans	Lime	Spices
Beets	Macadamia	Sprouts
Cauliflower	Mango	String Beans
Cabbage	Melon	Sunflower

Carrots	Mushrooms	Potatoes
Cashews	Oats	Tomatoes
Celery	Okra	Vegetable Oil
Cherries	Onion	Walnuts
Corn	Oranges	Whole Grains
Cucumber	Pears	Yams

Day 1 – Repentance

Scripture Reading: Proverbs Chapter 1-3 (Meditate on the Word of God).

"Then God saw everything that He had made, and indeed it was very good. So, the evening and the morning were the sixth day." (Genesis 1:31, NKJV).

When God completed His creation, everything was very good, nothing was missing, nothing was broken. It was all very good. This means you were created in perfection.

"I will praise You, for I am fearfully and wonderfully made; Marvelous are Your works, and that my soul knows very well." (Psalm 139:14, NKJV).

It is important to know that God created you in perfection. He designed you with awesomeness and uniqueness, creating you as a wonder. Everything in you was made right. You are God's masterpiece, made in His image and glory.

When sin was introduced, man fell from this state of perfection, and the glory departed. Sin created an open door for man to be afflicted with corruptibility. As such, man became susceptible to sickness and disease. Instead of enjoying the incorruptible nature that God has ordained for us, we now experience various sufferings, trials, and tribulations. What God created in perfection, now goes through various kinds of issues. I want you to understand that the same God who is in charge and created you in perfection is ready to bring restoration to your spirit, soul, and body. In the mighty name of Jesus Christ, total restoration is coming to you as you embark on this Ten-

15

Day Health Challenge, Daniel Fast, and Morning Battle Prayer.

"The Lord will perfect that which concerns me; Your mercy, O Lord, endures forever; Do not forsake the works of Your hands." (Psalm 138:8, NKJV).

Our God will not forsake the works of His hand. Remember you are His masterpiece.

In this hour, in this moment, I want you to cry out to God and repent from your ways. Repent from all the things you have done to your body and from all the things you have allowed into your mind. Say, "Lord I am sorry for neglecting this temple, for not taking proper care of this vessel. I am sorry O God for allowing so many things to enter me. Lord, I am sorry for my wrong eating habits.

I am sorry O God for not being diligent in caring for what You have entrusted to my care. I am sorry for adopting the mindset of the man who had one talent, the man who went and hid his talent. Lord, I do not want to hide the things You have given me. I desire to be in the optimum state in my life, O God. I want to be in good health, to enjoy wellness and wholeness. Today, Lord, I cry out to You and say, have mercy on me, O God."

"Lord, I have sinned against You in neglecting my body. I have sinned against You by not taking care of the temple of the Holy Spirit. I have sinned against You, O God, through my actions, the food I eat, through greed, and by being more food-conscious than heavenly-conscious. I have sinned by making food my idol."

For some people, food is their idol. In times of stress, upset, or need for comfort, they turn to food. "Father, I pray that you will have mercy on me."

Pray These Prayer Points:

- O Lord, have mercy on me in any areas where I have neglected the care of my body.
- O Lord, have mercy on me for being negligent in the affairs concerning my body.
  - For example, women often take great care of their appearance when going out. They apply makeup, dress stylishly, and present themselves well externally. However, despite their outward appearance, they may be facing inner struggles. Similarly, men might maintain physical fitness and wear the finest attire, yet internally, their bodies may be undergoing challenges. They might not be hydrating properly, exercising enough, or maintaining a balanced diet, neglecting essential supplements or herbs for their well-being. Despite looking attractive physically, their internal health might suffer, akin to a car with a flawless exterior but a malfunctioning engine. This does not align with God's intended wellness for us.
  - Cry out to God, and say, "O Lord, have mercy on me in any areas I have neglected the affairs of my body. Have mercy on me, O Lord, in any areas I have not tuned up my body. Have mercy on me, O Lord."
- O Lord, I repent from my sinful ways, and I forsake every bad eating habit.
- O Lord, I repent from bad food choices.
- I repent from greed when it comes to food.
- I repent from laziness when it comes to doing the right exercises to strengthen my body.
  - My body should represent You well.
  - My mind should represent You well.

- o   I am Christ's ambassador.

- I ask for all these things in Jesus' mighty name!

Make These Declarations:

Father, as I make these declarations, may Your light shine upon my ways in the name of Jesus Christ. Illuminate my health, O Lord. Show me the way and open my eyes to the path of life. Grant me knowledge, understanding, and wisdom. Help me in meditating on the wisdom of God and in gaining understanding from it.

- I decree and declare that my body is the temple of the Holy Spirit, as stated in 1 Corinthians 6:19, NKJV, **"Or do you not know that your body is the temple of the Holy Spirit who is in you, whom you have from God, and you are not your own?"**
- I decree and declare that my body will glorify God, in accordance with Matthew 5:16, NKJV, **"Let your light so shine before men, that they may see your good works and glorify your Father in heaven."**
- I decree and declare that my body is a living sacrifice unto the Lord, in accordance to Romans 12:1, NKJV, **"I beseech you therefore, brethren, by the mercies of God, that you present your bodies a living sacrifice, holy, acceptable to God, which is your reasonable service."**
- I decree and declare that my life will experience heavenly joy due to my commitment to repentance, as stated in Luke 15:10, NKJV, **"Likewise, I say to you, there is joy in the presence of the angels of God over one sinner who repents."**

- I decree and declare all these things in Jesus' mighty name!

"You will also declare a thing, and it will be established for you; So, light will shine on your ways." (Job 22:28, NKJV).

Communion:

Brothers and sisters, ladies, and gentlemen, as you partake in this communion, recognize its supernatural and powerful nature. What you are about to do is grounded in the Word of God. As you take this communion, you will receive healing, life, and regeneration. You are about to partake of communion, an act of worship that connects you to the heart of God.

"For I received from the Lord that which I also delivered to you: that the Lord Jesus on the same night in which He was betrayed took bread; and when He had given thanks, He broke it and said, "Take, eat; this is My body which is broken for you; do this in remembrance of Me." (1 Corinthians 11:23-24, NKJV).

Take the bread, break it, and say, "Father, as I take this bread, may Your body infuse mine with health."

"In the same manner He also took the cup after supper, saying, "This cup is the new covenant in My blood. This do, as often as you drink it, in remembrance of Me." For as often as you eat this bread and drink this cup, you proclaim the Lord's death till He comes." (1 Corinthians 11:25-26, NKJV).

"Lord, I thank You for Your precious blood. As I partake of Your precious blood, may it bring regeneration to every cell in my body, working a creative miracle in every part of my body. Renew my body, renew every organ, my heart, kidneys, liver, all the intestinal parts, eyesight, and brain cells, in the mighty name of Jesus Christ. Father, I thank You for the blood of Jesus. Through His sinless blood, I claim victory. Thank You, Father. I bless Your mighty name, seeking Your mercies to pour upon me. May my body manifest the benefits of communion. Make everything within me new! Restore health to my body and soul. You are the greatest Physician. Heal me, and I shall be healed. In Jesus' mighty name, Amen!"

Partake of His blood and give God thanks!

Concluding Prayer:

"O Lord, I thank You for all you have done for me, and I give You all the praise and glory. Precious Holy Spirit, grant me grace and revelation to abide by this Daniel Fast and follow the instructions in this book. As I seek restoration of my health, extend it to my wealth, spiritual growth, and development, Lord. Grant me blessings in every aspect. Thank You, Father! Thank You, Son! Thank You, precious Holy Spirit. May the face of the Lord shine upon me; may His glory rest upon me. In this season, I anticipate walking in double glory. As I continue this fast and adhere to its physical aspects, I commit to following the given instructions in these next ten days. Precious Holy Spirit, help me in this commitment, to honor and glorify You. All glory belongs to You; You alone deserve it. Thank You, Father. I bless and honor You. In Jesus' mighty name, Amen!"

PHYSICAL

Food: I recommend fasting from 6 am to 6 pm and breaking the fast with Daniel Fast meals. If you are taking medication, I suggest adhering to Daniel Fast for breakfast, lunch, and dinner. Refer to the section "Foods to Enjoy" for suggestions.

Drink: Drinking water significantly impacts your health. It aids your body's proper functioning and addresses many health concerns. The body relies on water to operate optimally. Some of the issues you have faced over the past couple of years may stem from insufficient hydration. You could be experiencing mild dehydration without realizing it, possibly attempting to resolve it through medications that do not address the root cause. Many of these problems could be attributed to mild dehydration. Trust in God as you prioritize water intake, as it can alleviate these issues. I understand that many prefer coffee, soda, or other less healthy beverages over water. However, during this health challenge and Daniel Fast, shifting to water intake will lead to noticeable improvements. Aim to drink an average of 8-12 cups a day (2 – 3 liters). Additionally, incorporating healthy, caffeine-free herbal teas or raw vegetable juice are good alternatives.

Exercise: "This is the day the Lord has made; We will rejoice and be glad in it." (Psalm 118:24, NKJV).

As today is the day the Lord has made, let us leap for joy by engaging in physical exercise. Commit to a minimum of 36.5 minutes of exercise, symbolizing 365 days in a year. You can choose activities like walking, dancing, running, jogging, swimming, biking, and more. Avoid remaining seated like idle individuals; instead, actively engage your body. Move around and participate in some form of exercise.

"Physical exercise has some value, but spiritual exercise is valuable in every way, because it promises life both for the present and for the future." (1 Timothy 4:8, GNT).

As you engage in this exercise, meditate on the Word of God.

One of the most challenging things is exercise. The 36.5 minutes is neither a magical nor mysterious number—it is a reminder to dedicate time to physical exercise for 365 days. Exercise is crucial; it prevents various sicknesses and diseases, reduces stress, promotes weight loss, and opens you up to receiving revelation from God.

From my personal experience, I have received revelations from the Lord while exercising. During my workouts, everything clears up. I am mentally sharp, receptive, and my hearing is clear. I strongly encourage you to embrace regular exercise. Skipping exercise and expecting to be ten times better is unrealistic. Physical exercise holds inherent value. Why not embrace that value for your betterment? do not allow old, negative thinking or an outdated mindset to deprive you of these benefits.

Day 2 – Break Free from Food Addictions

SPIRITUAL

Scripture Reading: Proverbs Chapter 4-6 (Meditate on the Word of God).

Today, you begin the journey to restoring your health to its perfect state. As you go through this process, believe God in God for miraculous testimonies. Food addiction is an area in our lives that the enemy has snuck into. We might not be addicted to alcohol or drugs, and praise God, as Princes unto the Lord, because we should avoid alcohol. And we might not be addicted to a crazy lifestyle either. However, the area where the enemy usually gains a great advantage is the area of food.

And some of us do not know it as an addiction. We say, "let me just enjoy the food" and "let me just eat it." Before we realize it, we might already be addicted, and it can affect us to the point where we become dependent on medication to survive. Medication may be relied on to sleep well at night and to alleviate the pain in our bodies. All of which can be attributed to food addiction. Today, food addiction is a silent killer in the body of Christ.

As you pray, believe that God will do a miracle in your body, breaking every addiction. Perhaps you have been dependent on medication or pharmaceutical drugs due to food addiction. I want you to trust that God will perform a miracle, and you will no longer need medication. I am not suggesting you stop your medication, but I am declaring that God will do a miracle in your body, and soon, you will not need it anymore.

23

The next time you visit your doctor, your doctor will check you and say that your cholesterol is correct, your blood pressure is normal, and you no longer have diabetes. Your doctor will be the one to take you off your medications.

Look at Daniel and his friends when they embarked on this journey. The Bible says after their ten-day trial, Daniel and his friends were examined, and they were found healthier, better, stronger, and as such, the chief eunuch released them to continue that diet. For three years, Daniel, Shadrach, and Abednego engaged in that diet. Brothers and sisters, ladies and gentlemen, our God is a good God. Believe God as you pray these prayers, believe that He will do a miracle in your life.

"All things are lawful for me, but all things are not helpful. All things are lawful for me, but I will not be brought under the power of any." (1 Corinthians 6:12, NKJV).

Though food is undoubtedly good for our nutritional value and development, it does not mean you should be addicted to it. Some individuals are addicted to sugar and sweet treats like cookies, chocolate, donuts… just name it. Others are addicted to meats such as fried chicken and red meat. You should know that too much of these foods can corrupt your body. Just because something is good and lawful, does not automatically make it the right thing to do. Today, you are going to break free from every addiction in the name of Jesus Christ.

Addiction is something that controls you, something that you cannot do without. It is something that you depend upon regardless of how harmful it is to your body, mental state, and emotional well-being.

24

When you are addicted to something, you lose control over its usage, becoming dependent on it. Take coffee, for instance. Many of us love coffee and can't do without it. Oh yes, we love coffee. Hallelujah!!! But now, for the next ten days, we must let go of coffee because it can be an addiction.

For instance, missing that cup of coffee might lead to headaches or dizziness, indicating an addiction that needs to be broken. We do not want to enslave ourselves to habits or substances, especially to the point where food begins to master us, affecting our bodies, thoughts, and movements.

Just imagine, before, when you could bend to pick up things without pain, but now, attempting to bend over causes discomfort. This is the result of letting food reshape your body. **That devil is a liar!** Today, you have every right to believe the Word of God and declare that this food addiction is coming to an end in the name of Jesus Christ. Pray that God will deliver you from the pain, effects, and consequences of the addiction on your body and mind. Trust that the God we serve will deliver you from it.

Pray These Prayer Points:

- My Father, deliver me from every root cause of food addiction in my life.
  - Is it a generational curse? Set me free today! In Jesus' name.
  - Is it family background? Set me free today! In Jesus' name.
  - Is it cultural background? Set me free today! In Jesus' name.
- I command the spirit of addiction to get out of my life. Addiction to food, addiction to nicotine, addiction to cigarettes, and addiction to alcohol.
  - I command you spirit of addiction to get out of my body in the mighty name of Jesus.
- I am healed from every emotional pain caused by addiction.
- I am healed from every side effect that affected my body due to addiction.
- O Lord, restore balance to every chemical and electrical frequency in my body.
- May every cell in my body produce healthy cells.
- I ask for all these things in Jesus' mighty name!

Make These Declarations:

I make these declarations by the power of the Holy Ghost and by the blood of Jesus Christ.

- I decree and declare that food will no longer be an addiction in my life. I will have a sound mind over food because according to 2 Timothy 1:7, NKJV,

"For God has not given us a spirit of fear, but of power and of love and of a sound mind."

- I decree and declare that in my life, there will be no more addiction to any form of liquid or substance. According to Galatians 5:22-23, NKJV, self-control is my portion, **"But the fruit of the Spirit is love, joy, peace, longsuffering, kindness, goodness, faithfulness, gentleness, self-control. Against such there is no law."**

- I decree and declare that my body will experience supernatural anti-aging. According to Joshua 14:10-11, NKJV, **"And now, behold, the LORD has kept me alive, as He said, these forty-five years, ever since the LORD spoke this word to Moses while Israel wandered in the wilderness; and now, here I am this day, eighty-five years old. As yet I am as strong this day as on the day that Moses sent me; just as my strength was then, so now is my strength for war, both for going out and for coming in."**

- I decree and declare that the spirit of addiction has no legal right over my body. My body is the temple of the Holy Spirit, which is stated in 1 Corinthians 6:19, NKJV, **"Or do you not know that your body is the temple of the Holy Spirit who is in you, whom you have from God, and you are not your own?"**

- I decree and declare that my body will glorify God for according to 1 Corinthians 6:20, NKJV, **"For you were bought at a price; therefore, glorify God in your body and in your spirit, which are God's."**

- I decree and declare all these things in Jesus' mighty name!

"You will also declare a thing, and it will be established for you; So, light will shine on your ways." (Job 22:28, NKJV).

Communion:

"Merciful Father, as I partake in this communion, pour out Your mercies upon me. May my body manifest the benefits of communion. Let everything within me become new! Restore health to my body and soul. You are the greatest Physician. Heal me, O God, and I shall be healed. In Jesus' mighty name, Amen!"

"For I received from the Lord that which I also delivered to you: that the Lord Jesus on the same night in which He was betrayed took bread; and when He had given thanks, He broke it and said, "Take, eat; this is My body which is broken for you; do this in remembrance of Me." (1 Corinthians 11:23-24, NKJV).

Take the bread, break it, and say, "Father, as I take this bread, may every addiction in my life be broken in the mighty name of Jesus."

"In the same manner He also took the cup after supper, saying, "This cup is the new covenant in My blood. This do, as often as you drink it, in remembrance of Me." For as often as you eat this bread and drink this cup, you proclaim the Lord's death till He comes." (1 Corinthians 11:25-26, NKJV).

Take the cup and say, "Father, as I take this cup, let Your precious blood cleanse my body from every addiction and let it release new blood cells, new organs, a new heart, a new kidney, new lungs, and let it renew the totality of my body in the mighty name of Jesus Christ! Amen!"

Partake of His blood and give God thanks!

Concluding Prayer

"Father, I thank You for healing and delivering me from food addiction. All glory and honor belong to You. I declare that food will no longer have dominion over me; I am free from the bondage of food. Thank You, Jesus, for restoring every chemical and electrical frequency in my body. May my ghrelin hormone function well, sending the right messages to my brain in the mighty name of Jesus. Every abnormality in my ghrelin and leptin hormones is now corrected in the mighty name of Jesus. I declare my freedom from food addiction in the mighty name of Jesus Christ. Amen!"

PHYSICAL

Food: I recommend fasting from 6 am to 6 pm and breaking the fast with Daniel Fast meals. If you are taking medication, I suggest adhering to Daniel Fast for breakfast, lunch, and dinner. Refer to the section "Foods to Enjoy" for suggestions.

Drink: Water is recommended. Aim to drink an average of 8-12 cups a day (2 – 3 liters). Healthy, caffeine-free herbal teas or raw vegetable juice are also good choices.

Exercise: "This is the day the Lord has made; We will rejoice and be glad in it." (Psalm 118:24, NKJV).

As today is the day the Lord has made, let us leap for joy by engaging in physical exercise. Commit to a minimum of 36.5 minutes of exercise, symbolizing 365 days in a year. You can choose activities like walking, dancing, running, jogging, swimming, biking, and more. Avoid remaining seated like idle individuals; instead, actively engage your body. Move around and participate in some form of exercise.

"Physical exercise has some value, but spiritual exercise is valuable in every way, because it promises life both for the present and for the future." (1 Timothy 4:8, GNT).

As you engage in this exercise, meditate on the Word of God.

Day 3 – New Heart – Detoxification

SPIRITUAL

Scripture Reading: Proverbs Chapter 7-10 (Meditate on the Word of God).

One of the most neglected areas when it comes to health and wellness is the heart. We tend to focus on every other area, but the main one—the heart—is left behind. The nucleus from which life's issues arise is not purified. Today, we are going to focus on the heart.

For you to become ten times better, to improve your health, be healed and freed from sickness and disease, you need to focus on your heart and present it to God.

"Keep your heart with all diligence, for out of it spring the issues of life." (Proverbs 4:23, NKJV).

"Above all else, guard your heart, for everything you do flows from it." (Proverbs 4:23, NIV).

Keeping your heart requires effort and attention. Guard it, protect it, keep it, and do not let toxic things infiltrate it. If everything we do flows from the heart, it means that it is crucial to nurture and ensure its well-being. Sometimes, during prayer, individuals may not fully engage their hearts, they go through the emotions, but their hearts are just simply not in it. Have you ever been in a relationship where the person's heart was not fully invested? You could sense that their heart was not in it. For some, their hearts are loaded with all kinds of things, making it heavy. do not let toxic things enter your heart. Many health issues stem from within, and that can lead to an infection, virus, or bacteria.

While undertaking spiritual detox, take this opportunity to engage in physical detox as well. Cleanse your body of chemicals through the detoxification process, and even consider incorporating herbal teas to aid in this endeavor.

"The heart is deceitful above all things, and desperately wicked; Who can know it?" (Jeremiah 17:9, NKJV).

"The heart is deceitful above all things, and it is extremely sick; Who can understand it fully and know its secret motives?" (Jeremiah 17:9, AMP).

The most deceitful thing in you is your heart. There are times where you may express that you are going to do something, but because your heart isn't in it, you do not get it done. Other times, you may plan to go somewhere, but because your heart isn't in it, you do not end up going.

Pray These Prayer Points:

- Heavenly Father, have mercy on me for neglecting my heart.
  - I come to You with a humble mind. Have mercy on me, O God.
  - Show me Your mercy and grant me Your salvation.
- My Father, detox my heart from every evil thing.
  - Purge my heart from every evil thing.
  - Purge my heart from every contamination.
- Father, detoxify my heart from all negativities.
- O Lord, test my heart according to Psalm 26:2, examining and proving me, **"Examine me, O**

LORD, and prove me; Try my mind and my heart."

- Reveal all that is not of You in my life, O Lord.
- Do surgery on my heart, O Lord. It says in Psalm 17:3, NKJV, **"You have tested my heart; You have visited me in the night; You have tried me and have found nothing; I have purposed that my mouth shall not transgress."**
  - o Once you give God permission to invade your privacy and to reveal those hidden things in your heart, you will be able to declare Psalm 17:3, NKJV, which says, **"You have tested my heart; You have visited me in the night; You have tried me and have found nothing; I have purposed that my mouth shall not transgress."**
  - o You have allowed God to visit your heart. You have allowed God to touch your heart.
- O Lord, create in me a clean heart.
  - o Psalm 51:10, NKJV, says, **"Create in me a clean heart, O God, and renew a steadfast spirit within me."**
  - o David realized that for him to overcome sin and the struggle of life, he needed a clean heart.
  - o Maybe your current heart has been causing sickness, pain, and disappointment. Today, you can cry out to God, and ask Him to create in you a clean heart, "Enough of that shattered heart. Enough of that broken heart. Enough of that wounded heart. O Father, create in me a clean heart."

- o For some of you, your hearts have been shattered over the past two years, maybe your heart has been broken the past three years, or even shattered the past seven years, and you are still carrying that pain along. Do you know that God specializes in healing the heart? This is the right time for you to cry out to God and say, "O Lord, create in me a clean heart."

- Jeremiah 29:12-13, NKJV, says, **"Then you will call upon Me and go and pray to Me, and I will listen to you. And you will seek Me and find Me when you search for Me with all your heart."**
  - o Going to the Lord with all your heart is a requirement. You cannot come to Him expecting transformation with only some of your heart.

- O Lord, remove iniquities from my heart. Psalm 66:18, NKJV, states **"If I regard iniquity in my heart, The Lord will not hear."**
  - o Some of you have regarded iniquity in your hearts for so long. It has become a comfort zone, a reference point. You can ask God to remove iniquity from your heart as you repent from your sins.

- Thank you, my Father, for granting me a pure heart. Psalm 24:3-4, NKJV, states **"Who may ascend into the hill of the LORD? And who may stand in His holy place? He who has clean hands and a pure heart, who has not lifted up his soul to falsehood and has not sworn deceitfully."**

- I ask for all these things in Jesus' mighty name!

Now that your heart is pure, I want you to start making these declarations.

Make These Declarations:

I make these declarations by the power of the Holy Ghost and by the blood of Jesus Christ.

- I decree and declare that I have a pure heart.
- I decree and declare that I have a new heart.
- I decree and declare that my heart will produce good things.
- I decree and declare that my heart will seek the Lord.
- I decree and declare that my heart will not be broken again.
- I decree and declare that my heart will be well.
- I decree and declare that my heart will experience wholeness.
- I decree and declare that my heart will have the heartbeat of my Heavenly Father.
- I decree and declare that my heart will beat with the right frequency.
- I decree and declare that my heart will be in sync with the heart of my heavenly Father.
- I decree and declare all these things in Jesus' mighty name!

"You will also declare a thing, and it will be established for you; So, light will shine on your ways." (Job 22:28, NKJV).

Communion

"I am the bread of life. Your fathers ate the manna in the wilderness and are dead. This is the bread which comes down from heaven, that one may eat of it and not die. I am the living bread which came down from heaven. If anyone eats of this bread, he will live forever; and the bread that I shall give is My flesh, which I shall give for the life of the world." (John 6:48-51, NKJV).

As you partake in communion, you are engaging in a supernatural act with this miraculous food. Today, as you take it, it will infuse your body, supercharge your system, boost your immune system, and bring about regeneration and recreation within you. It will restore your body to its natural state, eliminating every sickness and disease. I want you to believe in this. you are not merely fulfilling a religious duty; understand that this is holy before God. That's why, as you partake, do so with a pure and clean heart.

"For I received from the Lord that which I also delivered to you: that the Lord Jesus on the same night in which He was betrayed took bread; and when He had given thanks, He broke it and said, "Take, eat; this is My body which is broken for you; do this in remembrance of Me." (1 Corinthians 11:23-24, NKJV).

"Father, as I partake of Your body, let it infuse my body, Lord. May this be my immunization, my vaccination, and may it bring protection to my body. You promised that if I eat Your bread, I will not die. Let this supercharge my body. Keep death far from me. Let life and healing come to my body."

Partake of His body.

"In the same manner He also took the cup after supper, saying, "This cup is the new covenant in My blood. This do, as often as you drink it, in remembrance of Me." For as often as you eat this bread and drink this cup, you proclaim the Lord's death till He comes." (1 Corinthians 11:25-26, NKJV).

"Holy Father, thank You for the precious blood of Your Son, Jesus Christ, who knew no sin. As I partake of this precious blood, may it cleanse my heart and body of all toxicity, both spiritually and physically. May the blood of Jesus bring newness to my life. In Jesus' name, Amen!"

Partake of His blood and give God thanks!

Concluding Prayer:

"O Lord, thank You for purging my body from every unclean thing. Thank You for detoxifying my body, soul, and spirit. Thank You for manifesting Psalm 51:10 in my life. You have created in me a clean heart and you have renewed a steadfast spirit within me. My heart is purified and sanctified by the precious blood of Jesus Christ. In Jesus' mighty name. Amen!"

PHYSICAL

Food: I recommend fasting from 6 am to 6 pm and breaking the fast with Daniel Fast meals. If you are taking medication, I suggest adhering to Daniel Fast for breakfast, lunch, and dinner. Refer to the section "Foods to Enjoy" for suggestions.

37

Drink: Water is recommended. Aim to drink an average of 8-12 cups a day (2 – 3 liters). Healthy, caffeine-free herbal teas or raw vegetable juice are also good choices.

Exercise: "This is the day the Lord has made; We will rejoice and be glad in it." (Psalm 118:24, NKJV).

As today is the day the Lord has made, let us leap for joy by engaging in physical exercise. Commit to a minimum of 36.5 minutes of exercise, symbolizing 365 days in a year. You can choose activities like walking, dancing, running, jogging, swimming, biking, and more. Avoid remaining seated like idle individuals; instead, actively engage your body. Move around and participate in some form of exercise.

"Physical exercise has some value, but spiritual exercise is valuable in every way, because it promises life both for the present and for the future." (1 Timothy 4:8, GNT).

As you engage in this exercise, meditate on the Word of God.

Day 4 – Renew My Mind

SPIRITUAL

Scripture Reading: Proverbs Chapter 11-13 (Meditate on the Word of God).

"The mind governed by the flesh is death, but the mind governed by the Spirit is life and peace." (Romans 8:6, NIV).

As a child of God, you are at your best when you allow your mind to be governed by the Spirit of God instead of your flesh. When your mind is governed by the flesh, it leads to death, sickness, pain, and all kinds of undesirable outcomes. You may find yourself wondering, "why am I acting this way?" It is because your mind is being governed by the flesh. If your mind is controlled by the Spirit, you will have life, but if it is controlled by the flesh, it leads to death.

If your mind is unhealthy, it affects what your body produces and what your body is passionate about. When your mind is not healthy it affects your passion and your drive. For you to be effective, you must renew your mind daily with the Word of God and bring every thought captive to the obedience of Christ.

What sets us apart from unbelievers is that we have the Spirit of God within us. Allowing the Spirit of God to govern our lives reveals our identity as the sons of God. **"For as many as are led by the Spirit of God, these are sons of God."** (Romans 8:14, NKJV).

Brothers and sisters, there are some individuals who suffer from depression and their life is miserable. Did you know that depression is linked to mental health? When you experience depression, it indicates that your mental health is imbalanced, and it directly relates to the state of your mind. When your mind is not healthy, your mental health is affected.

There are those suffering from depression, schizophrenia, Bipolar Disorder, Anxiety Disorder, OCD, and PTSD. All these issues are linked to the mind—things you cannot see physically, hard to find with medical devices, yet they significantly impact the mind. While the heart is observable and can be examined, the mind is intangible. It takes the Spirit of God for examination and healing.

Today, I encourage you to pray for your mind. *Many of the battles you face in life are battles of the mind.* The mind is constantly at war with you, whispering discouragements and doubts: you are not good enough, you won't make it, no one wants to hear you, and so on. This mental struggle might be the reason some of you find it challenging to rise and move forward. Your mind might be telling you that you can't overcome challenges, lose weight, or be healed from sickness. *That devil is a liar!* Today, you are going to pray for the healing and restoration of your mind.

"And do not be conformed to this world, but be transformed by the renewing of your mind, that you may prove what is that good and acceptable and perfect will of God." (Romans 12:2, NKJV).

From this scripture, we understand that the renewal of your mind leads to transformation in your life. A renewed mind empowered you, making you effective in accomplishing things. It turns you into a catalyst for change. A healthy mind sharpens your discernment. Many of the mistakes we made in life were often due to our inability to discern the right path at the right time.

Pray These Prayer Points:

- My heavenly Father, I come with a humble heart, and I ask you to purge my mind from every dirty thing. Cleanse my mind from every negative thought.
- Precious Holy Spirit, I give You my mind, I surrender it to You.
- O Lord, let my mind have the consciousness of God!
- Passion and desire for food will no longer control my mind.
  - My mind will no longer be controlled by the dictate of the flesh, but instead, by the Spirit.
- Father, I pray, in the name of your Holy Son Jesus Christ, that every satanic or diabolical weapon formed towards my mind shall not prosper.
  - Have you ever heard that a person is crazy? This person is crazy because their mind is being controlled by satanic or diabolical forces.
  - If Satan can control your mind, he can control your body.
  - How can a human being, created in God's image and likeness, suddenly rip off his or her clothes and go homeless on the street? I am not talking about homelessness due to economic hardship. Some homeless people

out there have lost their minds—their minds are gone!

- The spell over your mind is broken in Jesus' mighty name.
  - o In certain situations, even after a relationship has ended, the influence of the person from that relationship may persist, and in a way, they still control you. For instance, you might find yourself going to bed with thoughts of them, and upon waking, they still occupy your mind. No matter where you go or what you are doing, they are always on your mind.
  - o Another example is when reminders of the person trigger flashbacks, which can be very unhealthy to your mental well-being. Many people deal with PTSD and anxiety because of this. And this is not uncommon among believers. Many believers deal with mental health issues, and most of these challenges are linked to the mind. To cope, one may attempt resorting to behaviors like relying on medication or overeating, however, such approaches do not work.
- I ask for all these things in Jesus' mighty name!

Make These Declarations:

I make these declarations by the power of the Holy Ghost and by the blood of Jesus Christ:

- I decree and declare I will get my mind back.
- I decree and declare that I will have the mind of Christ, for according to Philippians 2:5, NKJV,

which says, **"Let this mind be in you which was also in Christ Jesus,"**

- I decree and declare that my mind will produce good reports, positive thoughts, and pure and honorable things, for Philippians 4:8, NKJV, states, **"Finally, brethren, whatever things are true, whatever things are noble, whatever things are just, whatever things are pure, whatever things are lovely, whatever things are of good report, if there is any virtue and if there is anything praiseworthy—meditate on these things."**
- I decree and declare that my mind is empowered by the Holy Spirit.
- I decree and declare my mind is stable, well, and settled for according to 1 Peter 5:10, NKJV, **"But may the God of all grace, who called us to His eternal glory by Christ Jesus, after you have suffered a while, perfect, establish, strengthen, and settle you."**
- I decree and declare that my mind knows the truth and is free. John 8:32, NKJV, states **"And you shall know the truth, and the truth shall make you free."**
- I decree and declare all these things in Jesus' mighty name!

"You will also declare a thing, and it will be established for you; So, light will shine on your ways." (Job 22:28, NKJV).

Communion

As you partake in communion, you are engaging in a supernatural act with this miraculous food. Today, as you take it, it will infuse and supercharge your mind, renewing it from every satanic deposit. The mind of Christ will come alive in you, granting victory over every battle of the mind. You will rise and shine, becoming victorious. Understand that this isn't merely a religious duty; it is holy before God. That's why, as you partake, do so with a pure and clean heart.

"I am the bread of life. Your fathers ate the manna in the wilderness and are dead. This is the bread which comes down from heaven, that one may eat of it and not die. I am the living bread which came down from heaven. If anyone eats of this bread, he will live forever; and the bread that I shall give is My flesh, which I shall give for the life of the world." (John 6:48-51, NKJV).

"Father, as I partake of your body, let it infuse my mind, O Lord. Let this bring freedom and protection to my mind. You said if I eat your bread, I will not die. Let this supercharge my mind. Keep insanity, confusion, and brain fog far from me. Bring life and restoration to my mind. Your Word declares that by your stripes I am healed. Thank you, Father, for your broken body made available to me. In Jesus' mighty name. Amen!"

"For I received from the Lord that which I also delivered to you: that the Lord Jesus on the same night in which He was betrayed took bread; and when He had given thanks, He broke it and said, "Take, eat; this is My body which is broken for you; do this in remembrance of Me."" (1 Corinthians 11:23-24, NKJV).

44

Partake of His body

"In the same manner He also took the cup after supper, saying, "This cup is the new covenant in My blood. This do, as often as you drink it, in remembrance of Me." For as often as you eat this bread and drink this cup, you proclaim the Lord's death till He comes." (1 Corinthians 11:25-26, NKJV).

"Holy Father, thank You for the precious blood of Your Son, Jesus Christ, who knew no sin. As I partake of this precious blood, may it renew my mind and cleanse my body of all toxicity, both spiritually and physically. Let the blood of Jesus cleanse both my consciousness and subconsciousness of every toxic thought and imagination. May the blood of Jesus bring newness to my mind. In Jesus' name, Amen!"

Partake of His blood and give God thanks!

Concluding Prayer

"O Lord, thank You for purging my mind from every unclean thing. Thank You for renewing my mind with Your Word, as stated in Romans 12:2. I now possess a new mind, the mind of Christ within me, focusing on things above. According to Colossians 3:2, I am to set my mind on things above, not on earthly things. I walk in this new mindset through the precious blood of Jesus and the power of the Holy Spirit. In Jesus' mighty name. Amen!"

PHYSICAL

Food: I recommend fasting from 6 am to 6 pm and breaking the fast with Daniel Fast meals. If you are taking medication, I suggest adhering to Daniel Fast for breakfast, lunch, and dinner. Refer to the section "Foods to Enjoy" for suggestions.

Drink: Water is recommended. Aim to drink an average of 8-12 cups a day (2 – 3 liters). Healthy, caffeine-free herbal teas or raw vegetable juice are also good choices.

Exercise: "This is the day the Lord has made; We will rejoice and be glad in it." (Psalm 118:24, NKJV).

As today is the day the Lord has made, let us leap for joy by engaging in physical exercise. Commit to a minimum of 36.5 minutes of exercise, symbolizing 365 days in a year. You can choose activities like walking, dancing, running, jogging, swimming, biking, and more. Avoid remaining seated like idle individuals; instead, actively engage your body. Move around and participate in some form of exercise.

"Physical exercise has some value, but spiritual exercise is valuable in every way, because it promises life both for the present and for the future." (1 Timothy 4:8, GNT).

As you engage in this exercise, meditate on the Word of God.

Day 5 – Strengthen My Immune System

SPIRITUAL

Scripture Reading: Proverbs Chapter 14-16 (Meditate on the Word of God).

"For You formed my inward parts; You covered me in my mother's womb. I will praise You, for I am fearfully and wonderfully made; Marvelous are Your works, and that my soul knows very well. My frame was not hidden from You, When I was made in secret, and skillfully wrought in the lowest parts of the earth. Your eyes saw my substance, being yet unformed. And in Your book, they all were written, the days fashioned for me, when as yet there were none of them." (Psalm 139:13-16, NKJV).

Brothers and sisters, ladies, and gentlemen, it is God who formed you, putting everything together within you. When things are not in the right order, to whom do you turn? You turn to God, and He will set things right. Do not turn to the worldly system. You have every right to return to God. For he said, **"Before I formed you in the womb, I knew you; Before you were born, I sanctified you; I ordained you a prophet to the nations."** (Jeremiah 1:5, NKJV).

God was involved in forming Jeremiah. There is something special about humans: we have a built-in system known as the immune system. It is the engine that fights every attack on your body. When your immune system is strong, your body is strong. This holds true for both the physical and spiritual immune systems. When you fast, pray, or read the Word of God, you are building your spiritual immune

47

system. When spiritual attacks come, they won't shake you. You are already strong and know what to do. *That is your spiritual immune system.*

Often, we neglect our physical immune system, focusing our prayer on other things. Today, you are going to focus on your immune system. One of the ingredients to having divine health is having a good immune system. When your immune system is working at a hundred percent, you will begin to operate in divine health. When people claim to have divine health, it does not mean that sickness and disease do not attack their body. Rather, it signifies that when the attacks come, their body rejects it. It is an automatic rejection.

It is akin to when you send an email, and you receive an automatic response. It does not mean the person is right there typing a reply, it means that they set their email settings to send automatic responses. This is how your immune system operates. When an attack occurs, your immune system swiftly responds with "no!" I can imagine it is as if your immune system is making the following declaration, stating, "I know what I am made of. I know whose authority I obey, and therefore, you have no legal right to come in and dwell in this body." You have every right to dictate, declare, decree, pray and profess what your immune system will allow into your body.

As you make this declaration and seek His face, do it from a position of knowledge, from a position of knowing who you are in the Lord, from a position of knowing what His Word says about you, from a position of knowing who our God is and believing that He will do what no man can do and strengthen your immune system.

Pray These Prayer Points:

- Holy Father, every attack against my immune system, I nullify it in Jesus' mighty name.
  - For some, the reason they are not walking in ultimate health is because their immune system has been compromised.
- O Lord, expose every secret agent that is causing my immune system to be weak and disarm them of their power in the name of Jesus Christ.
- O Lord, correct every immunodeficiency in my body.
  - Correct every dysfunction in my immune system in Jesus' name.
- Precious Holy Spirit, empower my immune system to fight.
  - My immune system will do what it is supposed to do in the mighty name of Jesus Christ.
- Precious Holy Spirit, empower my immune system to resist the attacks of the enemies.
- Precious Holy Spirit, empower my immune system to destroy SAS COV-2, the virus that causes COVID-19.
- Precious Holy Spirit, empower my immune system to destroy the viruses that cause cancer.
- My Father, my Father, let the cells in my immune system be on red alert and destroy every intruder that does not belong in my body.
- O Lord, let my immune system reinforce the identity of my body for divine health.
- I ask for all these things in Jesus' mighty name!

Make These Declarations:

I make these declarations by the power of the Holy Ghost and by the blood of Jesus Christ.

- I decree and declare that my immune system is super charged by the Holy Spirit.
- I decree and declare that my immune system will not be compromised in Jesus' name.
- I decree and declare that no weapon formed against my immune system shall prosper according to Isaiah 54:17, NKJV, **"No weapon formed against you shall prosper, and every tongue which rises against you in judgment You shall condemn. This is the heritage of the servants of the LORD, and their righteousness is from Me," Says the LORD."**
- I decree and declare that I have the immune system of Jesus Christ because according to Galatians 2:20, NKJV, He lives in me, **"I have been crucified with Christ; it is no longer I who live, but Christ lives in me; and the life which I now live in the flesh I live by faith in the Son of God, who loved me and gave Himself for me."**
- I decree and declare that my immune system will line up with the Word of God.
- I decree and declare that my immune system has authority over sickness and diseases.
- I decree and declare that every cell in my body will work in perfect harmony with each other.
- I decree and declare all these things in Jesus' mighty name!

"You will also declare a thing, and it will be established for you; So, light will shine on your ways." (Job 22:28, NKJV).

Communion

As you partake in communion, know that you are engaging in a supernatural act, for this is a miraculous and divine food. When you take it today, it will supercharge your immune system and renew it from every satanic deposit. You are not merely fulfilling religious duty; understand that this is holy before God. Therefore, as you partake, do so with a pure and clean heart.

"I am the bread of life. Your fathers ate the manna in the wilderness and are dead. This is the bread which comes down from heaven, that one may eat of it and not die. I am the living bread which came down from heaven. If anyone eats of this bread, he will live forever; and the bread that I shall give is My flesh, which I shall give for the life of the world." (John 6:48-51, NKJV).

"Father, as I partake of your body, let it infuse my immune system, O Lord. May this bring freedom and protection to my immune system. You said if I eat your bread, I will not die. Let this supercharge and bring restoration to my immune system. Your Word declares that by Your stripes I am healed. Thank You, Father, for Your broken body made available to me. In Jesus' mighty name, Amen!"

"For I received from the Lord that which I also delivered to you: that the Lord Jesus on the same night in which He was betrayed took bread; and when He had given thanks, He broke it and said, "Take, eat; this is

My body which is broken for you; do this in remembrance of Me."" (1 Corinthians 11:23-24, NKJV).

Partake of His body

"In the same manner He also took the cup after supper, saying, "This cup is the new covenant in My blood. This do, as often as you drink it, in remembrance of Me." For as often as you eat this bread and drink this cup, you proclaim the Lord's death till He comes." (1 Corinthians 11:25-26, NKJV).

"Holy Father, thank you for the precious blood of Your Son, Jesus Christ, the blood that knew no sin. Lord, as I partake of Your precious blood, let it renew my immune system from every toxic thing. May it cleanse my consciousness and subconsciousness from every toxic thought and imagination. May it purify me spiritually and physically, bringing newness to my body. In Jesus' name, Amen!"

Partake of His blood and give God thanks!

Concluding Prayer

"O Lord, thank You for strengthening my immune system and correcting every immunodeficiency in my body. Precious Holy Spirit, empower my immune system to resist the attacks of the enemy. I give you all the glory, believing that weakness has no place in my body. Strength and power abound within me; my body is charged with the frequency of Your glory and might. In Jesus' name, Amen!"

PHYSICAL

Food: I recommend fasting from 6 am to 6 pm and breaking the fast with Daniel Fast meals. If you are taking medication, I suggest adhering to Daniel Fast for breakfast, lunch, and dinner. Refer to the section "Foods to Enjoy" for suggestions.

Drink: Water is recommended. Aim to drink an average of 8-12 cups a day (2 – 3 liters). Healthy, caffeine-free herbal teas or raw vegetable juice are also good choices.

Exercise: "This is the day the Lord has made; We will rejoice and be glad in it." (Psalm 118:24, NKJV).

As today is the day the Lord has made, let us leap for joy by engaging in physical exercise. Commit to a minimum of 36.5 minutes of exercise, symbolizing 365 days in a year. You can choose activities like walking, dancing, running, jogging, swimming, biking, and more. Avoid remaining seated like idle individuals; instead, actively engage your body. Move around and participate in some form of exercise.

"Physical exercise has some value, but spiritual exercise is valuable in every way, because it promises life both for the present and for the future." (1 Timothy 4:8, GNT).

As you engage in this exercise, meditate on the Word of God.

Day 6 – Long Life Is My Portion (Longevity)

SPIRITUAL

Scripture Reading: Proverbs Chapter 17-19 (Meditate on the Word of God).

"So, you shall serve the LORD your God, and He will bless your bread and your water. And I will take sickness away from the midst of you. No one shall suffer miscarriage or be barren in your land; I will fulfill the number of your days." (Exodus 23:25-26, NKJV).

Today, you are going to pray for a long life. Healthy longevity is your portion in Jesus' name. This promise is readily available to you, and you have the choice to align your life to receive this promise or not.

"Death and life are in the power of the tongue, and those who love it will eat its fruit." (Proverbs 18:21, NKJV).

Death and life are in the power of the tongue, offering you a choice in what you speak forth and the seeds you sow. The words that come out of your mouth are seeds and when those seeds are released, they will grow and yield fruit. When you sow the seed of long life, it will grow and bear forth the fruit of longevity.

As I previously mentioned, death and life are in the power of the tongue, which is why you are not wasting time when you engage in this kind of prayer. In fact, you may find yourself wishing you had started them earlier in life. Your current actions are setting the foundation for your future.

Your prayer is creating room for a divine turnaround because when you pray, there is always divine intervention. Today, your focus is on praying for longevity. We only have one life on earth because when we crossover, it will be for eternity. Why not make the best use of this life?

When you serve God, He makes the following promises:

- Bless your bread (some foods can be cursed).
- Bless your water (not all water is pure).
- Remove sickness from your midst.
- No miscarriage.
- No barrenness.
- Fulfillment of your destiny.

"With long life I will satisfy him and show him My salvation." (Psalm 91:16, NKJV).

He will satisfy you with a long life. Longevity is your portion. It is a promise!

"The silver-haired head is a crown of glory, if it is found in the way of righteousness." (Proverbs 16:31, NKJV).

"Gray hair is a crown of splendor; it is attained in the way of righteousness." (Proverbs 16:31, NIV).

"So, if you walk in My ways, to keep My statutes and My commandments, as your father David walked, then I will lengthen your days. Then Solomon awoke; and indeed, it had been a dream. And he came to Jerusalem and stood before the ark of the covenant of the Lord, offered up burnt offerings, offered peace offerings, and

made a feast for all his servants." (1 Kings 3:14-15, NKJV).

Your days on this earth can be lengthened or it can be shortened. Another example is Hezekiah.

"Children, obey your parents in the Lord, for this is right. "Honor your father and mother," which is the first commandment with promise: "that it may be well with you, and you may live long on the earth."" (Ephesians 6:1-3, NKJV).

Pray These Prayer Points:

- O Lord, have mercy on me in any areas I have not walked according to your ways.
- O Lord, forgive me if I have ever disobeyed my parents in the Lord.
- My Father, my Father, have mercy on me if I have not honored my father and mother.
- Precious Holy Spirit, help me to show honor.
- I cancel every premature death in the Name of Jesus'.
  - o It shall not be named among me.
  - o It shall not be named among my family.
- No evil power or forces shall cut my life short in the mighty name of Jesus.
- No death by accident, no death by incident in Jesus Name.

- I ask for all these things in Jesus' mighty name!

56

Make These Declarations:

I make these declarations by the power of the Holy Ghost and by the blood of Jesus Christ.

- I decree and declare that I will enjoy a healthy long life.
- I decree and declare that a healthy long life is my portion.
- I decree and declare that I will flourish according to Psalm 92:12, NKJV, **"The righteous shall flourish like a palm tree, He shall grow like a cedar in Lebanon."**
- I decree and declare that I will be a fruit bearer.
- I decree and declare that I will be fresh and flourishing in the name of Jesus.
- I decree and declare that the Spirit of God that manifested for Caleb will also manifest for me.
  - o I will have a strong spirit.
  - o **"And now, behold, the LORD has kept me alive, as He said, these forty-five years, ever since the LORD spoke this word to Moses while Israel wandered in the wilderness; and now, here I am this day, eighty-five years old."** (Joshua 14:10, NKJV).
  - o The Lord will keep me alive.
  - o The Lord will give me strength.
- I decree and declare longevity over my life in the name of Jesus.
- I decree and declare that I will not be weak or feeble.
- I decree and declare strength in my life.

- I decree and declare all these things in Jesus' mighty name!

"You will also declare a thing, and it will be established for you; So, light will shine on your ways." (Job 22:28, NKJV).

Communion

As you partake in communion, know that you are engaging in a supernatural act, for this is a miraculous and divine food. When you take it today, it will supercharge your longevity, anchoring you in life through Christ. You shall not die but live. This isn't merely a religious ritual to fulfill duty; recognize its holiness before God. Therefore, approach it with clean hands and a pure heart.

"I am the bread of life. Your fathers ate the manna in the wilderness and are dead. This is the bread which comes down from heaven, that one may eat of it and not die. I am the living bread which came down from heaven. If anyone eats of this bread, he will live forever; and the bread that I shall give is My flesh, which I shall give for the life of the world." (John 6:48-51, NKJV).

"Father, as I partake of your body, may longevity be my portion, O Lord. Let it bring life to my body, and may this heavenly bread be my daily sustenance. As I consume this holy bread, I declare victory over death through it; I shall not die but gain victory. Thank you, Father, for your broken body made available to me. In Jesus' mighty name, Amen!"

"For I received from the Lord that which I also delivered to you: that the Lord Jesus on the same night in which He was betrayed took bread; and when He had

given thanks, He broke it and said, "Take, eat; this is My body which is broken for you; do this in remembrance of Me."" (1 Corinthians 11:23-24, NKJV).

Partake of His body

"In the same manner He also took the cup after supper, saying, "This cup is the new covenant in My blood. This do, as often as you drink it, in remembrance of Me." For as often as you eat this bread and drink this cup, you proclaim the Lord's death till He comes." (1 Corinthians 11:25-26, NKJV).

"Holy Father, thank you for the precious blood of Your Son, Jesus Christ, for there is life in the blood. I have received the life in the blood of Jesus Christ, which has revitalized my mortal body. Through His blood, I have overcome blood-sucking demons and death. From now on, I will live in the abundant life that Christ has given me. In Jesus' name, Amen!"

Partake of His blood and give God thanks!

Concluding Prayer

"Father, I thank You, the author of life, for granting me the long life promised by You and the satisfaction that comes from Your promise. I declare that I shall not die but live to fulfill my destiny in Christ Jesus. Thank you for being the life-giver—no one can take the life You have granted me, no power of darkness can snatch it away. I am full of life and immortality is my portion. In Jesus' name, Amen!"

59

PHYSICAL

Food: I recommend fasting from 6 am to 6 pm and breaking the fast with Daniel Fast meals. If you are taking medication, I suggest adhering to Daniel Fast for breakfast, lunch, and dinner. Refer to the section "Foods to Enjoy" for suggestions.

Drink: Water is recommended. Aim to drink an average of 8-12 cups a day (2 – 3 liters). Healthy, caffeine-free herbal teas or raw vegetable juice are also good choices.

Exercise: "This is the day the Lord has made; We will rejoice and be glad in it." (Psalm 118:24, NKJV).

As today is the day the Lord has made, let us leap for joy by engaging in physical exercise. Commit to a minimum of 36.5 minutes of exercise, symbolizing 365 days in a year. You can choose activities like walking, dancing, running, jogging, swimming, biking, and more. Avoid remaining seated like idle individuals; instead, actively engage your body. Move around and participate in some form of exercise.

"Physical exercise has some value, but spiritual exercise is valuable in every way, because it promises life both for the present and for the future." (1 Timothy 4:8, GNT).

As you engage in this exercise, meditate on the Word of God.

Day 7 – Healing Is Mine

SPIRITUAL

Scripture Reading: Proverbs Chapter 20-22 (Meditate on the Word of God).

Brothers and sisters, ladies, and gentlemen, one of the benefits of Jesus' death on the cross is healing. When He died and rose again, we did not just receive salvation, we also received healing and deliverance.

"But unto you that fear My name shall the Sun of Righteousness arise with healing in His wings; and ye shall go forth and grow up as calves from the stall." (Malachi 4:2, KJV).

"But He was wounded for our transgressions, He was bruised for our iniquities; The chastisement for our peace was upon Him, And by His stripes we are healed." (Isaiah 53:5, NKJV).

This was before the death of Jesus Christ on the cross of Calvary. After His resurrection the scripture states the following:

"Who Himself bore our sins in His own body on the tree, that we, having died to sins, might live for righteousness—by whose stripes you were healed." (1 Peter 2:24, NKJV).

"Christ carried our sins in his body on the cross. He did this so that we would stop living for sin and live for what is right. By his wounds you were healed." (1 Peter 2:24, ERV).

"So, you shall serve the Lord your God, and He will bless your bread and your water. And I will take sickness away from the midst of you." (Exodus 23:25, NKJV).

Today, tap into the grace of healing as you read this chapter. By His wounds you were healed.

"Then your light shall break forth like the morning, your healing shall spring forth speedily, and your righteousness shall go before you; The glory of the LORD shall be your rear guard." (Isaiah 58:8, NKJV).

"He heals the brokenhearted and binds up their wounds." (Psalm 147:3, NKJV).

- He heals the brokenhearted.
- He binds up their wounds.

"He sent His word and healed them and delivered them from their destruction." (Psalm 107:20, NKJV).

It is your day to be delivered from every destructive sickness. It is your season to be delivered from every destructive sickness.

"So, you shall serve the Lord your God, and He will bless your bread and your water. And I will take sickness away from the midst of you." (Exodus 23:25, NKJV).

God promised to remove sickness from your midst. Believe God and His Word.

Pray These Prayer Points:

- Holy Father, take sickness away from me in the mighty name of Jesus according to Exodus 23:25, NKJV, **"So you shall serve the LORD your God, and He will bless your bread and your water. And I will take sickness away from the midst of you."**
- My Father, My Father, I believed in your Word, let my healings start now.
- O Lord, forgive me of my iniquities and heal me from all my diseases according to Psalm 103:3, NKJV, **"Who forgives all your iniquities, who heals all your diseases,"**
- Good Father, hear my cry today and heal me from my afflictions according to Psalm 30:2, NKJV, **"O LORD my God, I cried out to You, And You healed me."**
- Heal me, O Lord, and I shall be healed according to Jeremiah 17:14, NKJV, **"Heal me, O LORD, and I shall be healed; Save me, and I shall be saved, For You are my praise."**
- In the name of Jesus, I command my bones to receive healing.
- In the name of Jesus, I command my blood to receive healing.
- In the name of Jesus, I command every vital organ in my body to receive healing.
- In the name of Jesus, I command every cell in my body to receive healing.
- I ask for all these things in Jesus' mighty name!

Make These Declarations:

I make these declarations by the power of the Holy Ghost and by the blood of Jesus Christ.

- I decree and declare that I am healed by His stripes.
- I decree and declare that I am healed by His wounds.
- I decree and declare that every fiber of my being will hear the Word of the Lord.
- I decree and declare that my body is healed by the stripes of Jesus.
- I decree and declare that my soul is healed by the stripes of Jesus.
- I decree and declare that my spirit is healed by the stripes of Jesus.
- I decree and declare that my heart is healed.
- I decree and declare that my mind is healed.
- I decree and declare that my brain is healed.
- I decree and declare that my kidneys are healed.
- I decree and declare that my lungs are healed.
- I declare and declare that my liver is healed.
- I declare and declare that my pancreas is healed.
- I declare and declare that my intestines are healed.
- I decree and declare that every cell in my body will begin to function normally and function well.
- I decree and declare that this body will no longer know sickness.
- I decree and declare that this body will no longer know affliction.
- I decree and declare that this body is super charged by the power of the Holy Ghost.
- I decree and declare that sickness and disease will not touch my body.

- I decree and declare all these things in Jesus' mighty name!

"You will also declare a thing, and it will be established for you; So, light will shine on your ways." (Job 22:28, NKJV).

Communion

As you partake in this communion, it is crucial to recognize its supernatural and powerful nature, which aligns with the Word of God. Anticipate healing in your body as you take this communion, for it brings healing, life, and regeneration. This act of communion is an art of worship that connects you to the heart of God. Believe that your physical body will receive God's healing power and be restored to health and well-being.

"For I received from the Lord that which I also delivered to you: that the Lord Jesus on the same night in which He was betrayed took bread; and when He had given thanks, He broke it and said, "Take, eat; this is My body which is broken for you; do this in remembrance of Me."" (1 Corinthians 11:23-24, NKJV).

Take the bread, break it, and say, "Father, as I take this bread, let your body infuse my body with divine health."

"In the same manner He also took the cup after supper, saying, "This cup is the new covenant in My blood. This do, as often as you drink it, in remembrance of Me." For as often as you eat this bread and drink this cup, you proclaim the Lord's death till He comes." (1 Corinthians 11:25-26, NKJV).

"Lord, I thank You for Your precious blood. As I partake of Your precious blood, may it bring regeneration to every cell in my body, working a creative miracle in every part of my body. Renew my body, renew every organ, my heart, kidneys, liver, all the intestinal parts, eyesight, and brain cells, in the mighty name of Jesus Christ. Father, I thank You for the victorious power of the blood of Jesus, which knew no sin. Thank You, Father. I bless Your mighty name. Merciful Father, pour out Your mercies upon me. May my body manifest the benefits of communion and be renewed. Restore health to my body and soul. You are the greatest Physician, O Lord. Heal me and I shall be healed. In Jesus' mighty name, Amen!"

Partake of His blood and give God thanks!

Concluding Prayer:

"O Lord, I thank You for all You have done for me. Thank You for healing my body, a benefit I received by accepting Jesus Christ as my Lord and Savior. By His stripes, I am healed. Healing is mine, and all glory belongs to You. You alone deserve it. Thank You, Father. I bless and honor You. In Jesus' mighty name, Amen!"

PHYSICAL

Food: I recommend fasting from 6 am to 6 pm and breaking the fast with Daniel Fast meals. If you are taking medication, I suggest adhering to Daniel Fast for breakfast, lunch, and dinner. Refer to the section "Foods to Enjoy" for suggestions.

Drink: Water is recommended. Aim to drink an average of 8-12 cups a day (2 – 3 liters). Healthy, caffeine-free herbal teas or raw vegetable juice are also good choices.

Exercise: "This is the day the Lord has made; We will rejoice and be glad in it." (Psalm 118:24, NKJV).

As today is the day the Lord has made, let us leap for joy by engaging in physical exercise. Commit to a minimum of 36.5 minutes of exercise, symbolizing 365 days in a year. You can choose activities like walking, dancing, running, jogging, swimming, biking, and more. Avoid remaining seated like idle individuals; instead, actively engage your body. Move around and participate in some form of exercise.

"Physical exercise has some value, but spiritual exercise is valuable in every way, because it promises life both for the present and for the future." (1 Timothy 4:8, GNT).

As you engage in this exercise, meditate on the Word of God.

Day 8 – Fasting Can

SPIRITUAL

Scripture Reading: Proverbs Chapter 23-25 (Meditate on the Word of God).

"But put on the Lord Jesus Christ, and make no provision for the flesh, to fulfill its lusts." (Romans 13:14, NKJV).

"And when they had come to the multitude, a man came to Him, kneeling down to Him and saying, "Lord, have mercy on my son, for he is an epileptic and suffers severely; for he often falls into the fire and often into the water. So, I brought him to Your disciples, but they could not cure him." Then Jesus answered and said, "O faithless and perverse generation, how long shall I be with you? How long shall I bear with you? Bring him here to Me." And Jesus rebuked the demon, and it came out of him; and the child was cured from that very hour. Then the disciples came to Jesus privately and said, "Why could we not cast it out?" So, Jesus said to them, "Because of your unbelief; for assuredly, I say to you, if you have faith as a mustard seed, you will say to this mountain, 'Move from here to there,' and it will move; and nothing will be impossible for you. However, this kind does not go out except by prayer and fasting." (Matthew 17:14-21, NKJV).

This kind does not go away except by prayer and fasting. I do not know what kind of stubborn situation you are dealing with… what stubborn sickness or affliction that is still in your life. Some of you have been praying, and those problems still persist. Similar to the disciples in Matthew chapter 10, where they accomplished great things (demons fled, people were healed, and people rejoiced). However, in chapter 17, we see that the disciples found it difficult to deliver a boy from the oppression of the devil. Jesus told them that this kind does not go out except through prayer and fasting.

Every stubborn situation disturbing your body, every stubborn situation the enemies have assigned against your health, must give way today because **fasting can also be in the name of Jesus of Christ.**

The Benefits of Fasting:

- Fasting is a requirement for our spiritual development.
- When you fast, your heavenly Father will reward you openly – The result of a true godly fast brings about physical manifestation of the blessings of God.
- Fasting helps you humble your soul before the almighty God according to Psalm 35:13, NKJV, **"But as for me, when they were sick, my clothing was sackcloth; I humbled myself with fasting; And my prayer would return to my own heart."**
- Fasting helps you put the flesh in proper perspective. It brings life to your spirit.
- Fasting helps us put the flesh in check so that the spirit of God will rise in us according to Galatians 5:24, NKJV, **"And those who are Christ's have crucified the flesh with its passions and desires."**

Galatians 6:8, NKJV, **"For he who sows to his flesh will of the flesh reap corruption, but he who sows to the Spirit will of the Spirit reap everlasting life."**

- Fasting is a spiritual tool that helps break free from bondage.
- Fasting reveals the stronghold that is working against your destiny.
- Fasting prepares your spirit to receive revelation from God.
- Fasting gives room for divine intervention.
- Fasting brings supernatural breakthroughs.
- Fasting releases God's healing power.

What is that stubborn situation in your life? There are things you want to do to enhance your well-being, but you find yourself unable to proceed. You start but then stop, unable to move forward. There are issues in your body that come and go, persisting despite your efforts.

But today, in the name of Jesus, you will confront that stubborn situation. You will stand against that persistent spirit in the Name of Jesus Christ. Today marks your deliverance from stubborn demons through fasting. In Christ Jesus, you hold the authority to confront every persistent demon that has hindered your progress.

I pray that the power of the Holy Spirit will come upon you and cast out every stubborn demon. He will cast out that thing that has been disturbing your peace, that thing that has been disturbing your sleep, that thing that has been disturbing your joy. The power of the Holy Ghost is coming upon you for a change in your life.

Let me remind you about the authority you have in Christ Jesus.

"Then He called His twelve disciples together and gave them power and authority over all demons, and to cure diseases." (Luke 9:1, NKJV).

I want you to know that authority belongs to you because Christ has given it to you. **"Most assuredly, I say to you, he who believes in Me, the works that I do he will do also; and greater works than these he will do, because I go to My Father."** (John 14:12, NKJV).

The authority of our Lord Jesus Christ is upon you. It is your right to execute it and exercise it. That is what you are going to do. **"… For this purpose, the Son of God was manifested, that He might destroy the works of the devil."** (1 John 3:8, NKJV).

What you are going to do today is to dismantle the works of the devil that have been influencing your life, your marriage, your health, and your children. Today marks its end. It will expire by the fire of the Holy Ghost.

Pray These Prayer Points:

- In the name of Jesus Christ, my light will shine.
    - I call forth for the light in me to shine. When the light in me shines, darkness will flee.
    - I pray that there will be no room for darkness in my life. Darkness serves as an entry point for demons to gain access to my life. Therefore, in Jesus' mighty name, I eradicate every trace of darkness from my life.

71

- Every demonic influence working against my health, I cast it out in the mighty name of Jesus.
- I am released from every demonic stronghold, in the mighty name of Jesus.
  - O Lord, I am freed from my infirmity.
- Jesus said to them, this kind can only be done through prayer and fasting.
  - O Lord, based on my prayer and fasting, I make my supplication, I make my request: I am released from every spirit of infirmity in the name of Jesus Christ.
- My Father, my Father, every plant that you have not planted in me, I uproot it in the mighty name of Jesus in accordance with Matthew 15:13, NKJV, **"But He answered and said, "Every plant which My heavenly Father has not planted will be uprooted."**
- O Lord, nullify every plan of the enemies against my body according to Isaiah 7:7, NKJV, **"thus says the Lord GOD: "It shall not stand, nor shall it come to pass."**
  - Do you know the enemy is always sending things against believers? That is the reason the Bible calls him the "accuser of the brethren that accuses them day and night."
  - The accuser has no legal right over my body or my life, not in my body, not in my life.
- I command every demonic or satanic weapon formed against my body to scatter in Jesus' name.
- By the fire of the Holy Spirit, I quench every flaming missile or fiery darts directed towards my body in Jesus' mighty name.
- I ask for all these things in Jesus' mighty name!

Make These Declarations:

I make this declaration by the power of the Holy Ghost and by the blood of Jesus Christ.

- I command every spirit of sickness to come out of my body.
  - Out of my body, out of my mind.
- I command every spirit of unforgiveness to come out of me.
  - Out of my body, out of my mind.
- I command every spirit of anger to come out of me.
  - Out of my body, out of my mind.
- I command every spirit of fear to come out of me.
  - Out of my body, out of my mind.
- I command every spirit of selfishness to come out of me.
  - Out of my body, out of my mind.
- I command every spirit of bitterness to come out of me.
  - Out of my body, out of my mind.
- I command every spirit of affliction to come out of me.
  - Out of my body, out of my mind.
- I command every spirit of chemical imbalance to come out of me.
  - Out of my body, out of my mind.
- I command every spirit of hatred to come out of me.
  - Out of my body, out of my mind.
- I command every hot temper to come out of me.
  - Out of my body, out of my mind.
- I command every stubborn spirit to come out of me.
  - Out of my body, out of my mind.

- I command the spirit of disobedience to come out of me.
  - Out of my body, out of my mind.
- I command the spirit of restlessness to come out of me.
  - Out of my body, out of my mind.
- I command the spirit of confusion to come out of me.
  - Out of my body, out of my mind.
- I command the spirit of disorder to come out of me.
  - Out of my body, out of my mind.
- I command PTSD to come out of me.
  - Out of my body, out of my mind.
- I command OCD to come out of me.
  - Out of my body, out of my mind.
- I command every drug to come out of me.
  - Out of my body, out of my mind.
- I command every vaccine to come out of me.
  - Out of my body, out of my mind.
- I command envy to come out of me.
  - Out of my body, out of my mind.
- I command suicide to come out of me.
  - Out of my body, out of my mind.
- I command death to come out of me.
  - Out of my body, out of my mind.
- I command insomnia to come out of me.
  - Out of my body, out of my mind.
- I command insanity to come out of me.
  - Out of my body, out of my mind.
- I command retardation to come out of me.
  - Out of my body, out of my mind.
- I command paranoia to come out of me.
  - Out of my body, out of my mind.

- I command hallucination to come out of me.
  - Out of my body, out of my mind.
- I command forgetfulness to come out of me.
  - Out of my body, out of my mind.
- I command greed to come out of me.
  - Out of my body, out of my mind.
- I command irritability to come out of me.
  - Out of my body, out of my mind.
- I command the spirit of frustration to come out of me.
  - Out of my body, out of my mind.
- I command sadness and sorrow to come out of me.
  - Out of my body, out of my mind.
- I command bad dreams to come out of me.
  - Out of my body, out of my mind.
- I command every spirit of condemnation to come out of me.
  - Out of my body, out of my mind.
- I command chronic sickness to come out of me.
  - Out of my body, out of my mind.
- In the name of Jesus Christ!!!
- I decree and declare that I will work in dominion authority according to Jeremiah 1:10, NKJV, **"See, I have this day set you over the nations and over the kingdoms, to root out and to pull down, To destroy and to throw down, To build and to plant."**
- I fill every space in my life with the Fruits of the Spirit according to Galatians 5:22-23, NKJV, **"But the fruit of the Spirit is love, joy, peace, longsuffering, kindness, goodness, faithfulness, gentleness, self-control. Against such there is no law."**

- Thank you, O Lord! I am free, I am free, I am free. In Jesus' name.
- I decree and declare all these things in Jesus' mighty name!

"You will also declare a thing, and it will be established for you; So, light will shine on your ways." (Job 22:28, NKJV).

Communion:

"Merciful Father, as I partake in this communion, pour out Your mercy upon me. May my body manifest the benefits of communion and fasting. May every stubborn demon, issue, and circumstance bow to the name of Jesus Christ. Bring about a supernatural turnaround in my life and circumstances. In Jesus' mighty name, Amen!"

"For I received from the Lord that which I also delivered to you: that the Lord Jesus on the same night in which He was betrayed took bread; and when He had given thanks, He broke it and said, "Take, eat; this is My body which is broken for you; do this in remembrance of Me." (1 Corinthians 11:23-24, NKJV).

Take the bread, break it, and say, "Father, as I take this bread, let your body infuse my body with divine turnaround."

"In the same manner He also took the cup after supper, saying, "This cup is the new covenant in My blood. This do, as often as you drink it, in remembrance of Me." For as often as you eat this bread and drink this cup, you proclaim the Lord's death till He comes." (1 Corinthians 11:25-26, NKJV).

"Lord, I thank You for Your precious blood. As I partake of it, may it bring regeneration to every cell in my body and work a creative miracle in every part of me. May Your blood activate supernatural restoration in my body, soul, and spirit. Thank You, Father. I bless Your mighty name, O Lord. Merciful Father, pour out Your mercies upon me. May my body manifest the benefits of communion and fasting, experiencing complete renewal. In Jesus' mighty name, Amen!"

Partake of His blood and give God thanks!

Concluding Prayer:

"Father, I thank You for delivering me and setting me free from every stubborn situation. I stand firm upon the truth in Your Word. The truth I believe and receive has granted me freedom. Thank You for the liberty, Christ made available to me. I will walk in this newfound freedom and will not be hindered in Jesus' mighty name, Amen!"

PHYSICAL

Food: I recommend fasting from 6 am to 6 pm and breaking the fast with Daniel Fast meals. If you are taking medication, I suggest adhering to Daniel Fast for breakfast, lunch, and dinner. Refer to the section "Foods to Enjoy" for suggestions.

Drink: Water is recommended. Aim to drink an average of 8-12 cups a day (2 – 3 liters). Healthy, caffeine-free herbal teas or raw vegetable juice are also good choices.

Exercise: "This is the day the Lord has made; We will rejoice and be glad in it." (Psalm 118:24, NKJV).

As today is the day the Lord has made, let us leap for joy by engaging in physical exercise. Commit to a minimum of 36.5 minutes of exercise, symbolizing 365 days in a year. You can choose activities like walking, dancing, running, jogging, swimming, biking, and more. Avoid remaining seated like idle individuals; instead, actively engage your body. Move around and participate in some form of exercise.

"Physical exercise has some value, but spiritual exercise is valuable in every way, because it promises life both for the present and for the future." (1 Timothy 4:8, GNT).

As you engage in this exercise, meditate on the Word of God.

Day 9 – My Time of Restoration

SPIRITUAL

Scripture Reading: Proverbs Chapter 26-28 (Meditate on the Word of God).

Brothers and sisters, ladies, and gentlemen, today is your day to pray for restoration. After healing comes restoration, and when affliction is over, restoration comes.

"After Job had prayed for his friends, the LORD restored his fortunes and gave him twice as much as he had before." (Job 42:10, NIV).

The Lord restored to Job his losses. Who did it? God did it! Today, you are going to believe God that the same God who restored Job's health will also bring restoration to your life.

"So, I will restore to you the years that the swarming locust has eaten, the crawling locust, The consuming locust, And the chewing locust, My great army which I sent among you." (Joel 2:25, NKJV).

This was a prophetic declaration. The Lord says, **"I will restore to you the years."** Some of you have lost time due to sickness, health issues, or other difficult circumstances, but I am here to tell you that we serve a God who can restore not only your health but also your lost time. I encourage you to believe that, as you pray, Almighty God will make it happen for you and your family.

"Restore us, O God; Cause Your face to shine, and we shall be saved!" (Psalm 80:3, NKJV).

Only God can restore, not man. What is it that is missing in your life? What is it that has been stolen from you? You can declare: **"Restore us, O Lord God of hosts; Cause Your face to shine, and we shall be saved!"** (Psalm 80:19, NKJV).

This phrase was so powerful, the Psalmist repeated it a couple of times in Psalm 80:3, Psalm 80:19, and in Psalm 85:4: **"Restore us, O God of our salvation, and cause Your anger toward us to cease."** (Psalm 85:4 NKJV).

Brothers and sisters, the God that saved you and delivered you is the same God and He is able to restore you.

What is awesome about God? What is good about God? What is great about God? Well, when God restores, He makes it better than before. Take a look at Job; God gave him double! The Bible also says that the Hebrew boys were ten times better. As you pray, I want you to believe that the restoration you are going to receive will be ten times better.

The Bible says **"The thief comes only to steal, kill and destroy. I came that they may have life, and have it in abundance [to the full, till it overflows]."** (John 10:10, AMP).

When God restores, it is an overflow restoration.

"Yet when he is found, he must restore sevenfold; He may have to give up all the substance of his house." (Proverbs 6:31, NKJV).

Whoever stole your health, whoever stole your peace, whoever stole your joy, whoever stole your marriage, shall restore it today. Today is your day of restoration.

"The LORD will restore the splendor of Jacob like the splendor of Israel, though destroyers have laid them waste and have ruined their vines." (Nahum 2:2, NIV).

Today, as you pray, God will bring restoration to you. I may not know what the destroyer has caused in your life or what it has laid waste to but hear the Word of the Lord: restoration is coming!

Pray These Prayer Points:

- My Father, restore to me the joy of my salvation according to Psalm 51:12, NKJV, **"Restore to me the joy of Your salvation, and uphold me by Your generous Spirit."**
  - As I rejoice in You, let health manifest for me.
  - Let my laughter become medicine to my soul.
- O Lord, restore health to me according to Jeremiah 30:17, NKJV, **"For I will restore health to you and heal you of your wounds,' says the LORD, 'Because they called you an outcast saying: "This is Zion; No one seeks her."**
- Father, as I pray, whoever stole my health, let them restore it to me now in Jesus' mighty name.
  - Whoever has stolen my destiny, whoever has stolen my wealth, whoever has stolen my life, I command them to restore it today or die.
  - I put a demand on the spiritual realm. I command every satanic and diabolical force holding my destiny hostage, holding my

health hostage, holding my life hostage, and holding my wellness hostage to restore it. By the authority and in the name of our Lord Jesus Christ, I decree and declare for them to restore it today or die, by the fire of the Holy Ghost.

- o I call down the fire of God over every thief and every destroyer holding my destiny hostage, holding my health hostage, and holding my breakthrough hostage. I decree fire, fire, fire, fire, fire, fire, fire, fire, fire, fire! In the name of Jesus.
- o Restore my health, restore my blessing, restore my dignity, restore my identity. Today, restore it all in the name of Jesus. Let go!

- O Lord, destroy the destroyer and restore my splendor according to Nahum 2:2, NIV, **"The LORD will restore the splendor of Jacob like the splendor of Israel, though destroyers have laid them waste and have ruined their vines."**
- O Lord, show me your kindness today and let my inheritance be restored.
  - o My inheritance will be restored.
- O Lord, let my possessions be restored according to your Word in Nehemiah 5:11, NKJV, **"Restore now to them, even this day, their lands, their vineyards, their olive groves, and their houses, also a hundredth of the money and the grain, the new wine and the oil, that you have charged them."**

Make These Declarations:

I make these declarations by the power of the Holy Ghost and by the blood of Jesus Christ.

- I decree and declare that my health is restored.
- I decree and declare everything in me is restored according to God's divine order.
- I decree and declare in the name of Jesus that my joy is restored.
- I decree and declare that my mind is restored.
- I decree and declare that my soul is restored.
- I decree and declare that in the name of Jesus that my glory is restored.
- I decree and declare that my blessings are restored.
- I decree and declare in the name of Jesus everything stolen from me by the enemies are restored.
- I decree and declare in the name of Jesus everything stolen from me by the pandemic are restored.
- I decree and declare that my time is restored.
- I decree and declare that my life is restored.
- I decree and declare that my family is restored.
- I decree and declare that restoration is my portion.
- I decree and declare that the favor of God is restored all over me.
- I decree and declare double glory.
- I decree and declare glory to glory.
- I decree and declare grace to grace.
- I decree and declare all these things in Jesus' mighty name!

"You will also declare a thing, and it will be established for you; So, light will shine on your ways." (Job 22:28, NKJV).

Communion

"Merciful Father, as I partake in this communion, pour out Your mercies upon me. May this mark the beginning of a total and complete restoration in my life. Grant me all-around restoration. Whatever has been stolen from me shall be restored. In Jesus' mighty name, Amen!"

"For I received from the Lord that which I also delivered to you: that the Lord Jesus on the same night in which He was betrayed took bread; and when He had given thanks, He broke it and said, "Take, eat; this is My body which is broken for you; do this in remembrance of Me."" (1 Corinthians 11:23-24, NKJV).

Take the bread, break it, and say, "Father, as I take this bread, let restoration start in my life now."

"In the same manner He also took the cup after supper, saying, "This cup is the new covenant in My blood. This do, as often as you drink it, in remembrance of Me." For as often as you eat this bread and drink this cup, you proclaim the Lord's death till He comes." (1 Corinthians 11:25-26, NKJV).

"Lord, I thank You for Your precious blood. As I partake of it, may it bring restoration to my life now. May your blood activate supernatural restoration in my body, soul, and spirit. Thank You, Father. In Jesus' mighty name, Amen!"

Partake of His blood and give God thanks!

Concluding Prayer:

"Holy Father, my heart is full of your love and generosity of your grace towards my life. Your mercy has opened the realm of restoration over my life. Therefore, I believe and declare that everything stolen from me shall be restored. In Jesus' mighty name, Amen!"

PHYSICAL

Food: I recommend fasting from 6 am to 6 pm and breaking the fast with Daniel Fast meals. If you are taking medication, I suggest adhering to Daniel Fast for breakfast, lunch, and dinner. Refer to the section "Foods to Enjoy" for suggestions.

Drink: Water is recommended. Aim to drink an average of 8-12 cups a day (2 – 3 liters). Healthy, caffeine-free herbal teas or raw vegetable juice are also good choices.

Exercise: "This is the day the Lord has made; We will rejoice and be glad in it." (Psalm 118:24, NKJV).

As today is the day the Lord has made, let us leap for joy by engaging in physical exercise. Commit to a minimum of 36.5 minutes of exercise, symbolizing 365 days in a year. You can choose activities like walking, dancing, running, jogging, swimming, biking, and more. Avoid remaining seated like idle individuals; instead, actively engage your body. Move around and participate in some form of exercise.

"Physical exercise has some value, but spiritual exercise is valuable in every way, because it promises life both for the present and for the future." (1 Timothy 4:8, GNT).

As you engage in this exercise, meditate on the Word of God.

Day 10 – Thanksgiving

SPIRITUAL

Scripture Reading: Proverbs Chapter 29-31 (Meditate on the Word of God).

Brother and sister, ladies and gentlemen, thanksgiving is our secret weapon to get things done. Never forget the power of thanksgiving to activate the supernatural. Thanksgiving unlocks the heavenly gates. Thanksgiving is the password into the supernatural. Today, you are going to deploy your spiritual tool of thanksgiving to conclude this Ten-Day Health Challenge, Daniel Fast and Morning Battle Prayer.

Whatever you do, learn to start, and end it with thanksgiving. Thanksgiving is a secret weapon that you need to deploy in your life. Often, we focus on various aspects of worship, like prayer, but there is incredible power in thanksgiving that is often overlooked.

Thanksgiving is when you are full of gratitude, deeply appreciative for all that God has done for you and the things He has in store for you. Even for things you have not even seen yet, you are grateful and rejoicing. Thanksgiving is the heart of gratitude and gratefulness. Just by waking up in the morning, being able to breathe in oxygen, is enough for you to say, "Father, thank you for today." You should rise from the bed with thanksgiving in your heart and make a simple declaration like, "Father, I thank you for the dawning of a new day. I am going to have a glorious day. Thank you, Father!"

86

The prayer you will offer today is poised to transform your life into one of gratitude. As you consistently embrace thanksgiving, it evolves from a practice to a lifestyle. Giving thanks becomes effortless; it naturally flows from your heart. It is no longer merely part of prayer; it becomes a powerful tool in its own right.

When you are out and about, a simple "thank you, Lord" can suffice. At the grocery store, in response to a call or mail, or when faced with a troubling situation like a bill, cultivate the habit of saying "thank you, Father." Let thanksgiving become second nature. Instead of stress, respond with gratitude. When tempted to complain or curse, let thanksgiving flow. That's the transformation you should aim for.

I believe that as you go through this book and engage in fasting and prayer, you will develop an unprecedented habit of giving thanks to God.

People might think you are crazy, but we know the God that we serve.

"Enter into His gates with thanksgiving, And into His courts with praise. Be thankful to Him and bless His name." (Psalm 100:4, NKJV).

"One of them, when he saw that he was healed, turned back, glorifying and praising and honoring God with a loud voice; and he lay face downward at Jesus' feet, thanking Him [over and over]. He was a Samaritan. Then Jesus asked, "Were not ten [of you] cleansed? Where are the [other] nine? Was there no one found to return and to give thanks and praise to God, except this foreigner?" Jesus said to him, "Get up and go [on your way]. Your faith [your personal trust in Me and your

confidence in God's power] has restored you to health." (Luke 17:15-19, AMP).

Today, you are going to proclaim with the voice of thanksgiving the blessings of God over your life. With the voice of thanksgiving, declare your health and wellness.

"That I may proclaim with the voice of thanksgiving and tell of all Your wondrous works." (Psalm 26:7, NKJV).

Utilize the voice of thanksgiving as you engage in the following prayer points. These are straightforward yet impactful points designed to reprogram your mind and activate a heart of gratitude within you. It moves beyond a mere form of prayer; it becomes an integral part of who you are.

Pray These Prayer Points:

- Father, I thank you for the life you have given unto me.
- Father, I thank you for the precious Holy Spirit.
  - When you are thankful for the Holy Spirit, you become conscious of the Holy Spirit.
- Father, I thank you for my salvation.
- Father, I thank you for my deliverance.
- Father, I thank you for delivering me from the hands of my enemies.
- Father, I thank you for good health.
- Father, I thank you for healing me.
  - Thank you for healing my body.
- Father, I thank you for removing shame from my life.

88

- Father, I thank you for protecting me, day and night.
- Father, I thank you for sustaining my life.
- Father, I thank you for allowing goodness and mercy to follow me.

- I ask for all these things in Jesus' mighty name!

Make These Declarations:

I make these declarations by the power of the Holy Ghost and by the blood of Jesus Christ.

- I decree and declare that my mouth will give you thanks.
- I decree and declare that my soul will give you thanks.
- I decree and declare that thanksgiving will be my daily language.
- I decree and declare that in the morning I will give you thanks.
- I decree and declare that at noon I will give you thanks.
- I decree and declare that in the evening I will give you thanks.
- I decree and declare that in the midnight hour I will give you thanks.
- I decree and declare that I am ten times better:
  - In my spiritual gifts, I will become ten times better.
  - In my net worth, I will become ten times better.
  - In my prayer life, I will become ten times better.
  - In my value, I will become ten times better.

89

- o In my marriage, I will become ten times better.
- o In my family, I will become ten times better.
- o In my life, I will become ten times better.
- o Ten times better anointing will begin to work for me.
- o God will give me ten times increase.
- o God will enlarge my dream ten times.
- o God will enlarge my territory ten times better.
- o I decree and declare all these things in Jesus' mighty name!

"You will also declare a thing, and it will be established for you; So, light will shine on your ways." (Job 22:28, NKJV).

Communion:

"Merciful Father, as I partake in this communion, pour out Your mercies upon me. May my body manifest the benefits of this communion. Renew everything within me! Restore health to my body and soul. You are the greatest Physician. Heal me, and I shall be healed. In Jesus' mighty name, Amen!"

As you partake in this communion, take a moment to give thanks to God. Let this communion be an expression of gratitude. Offer thanks to God with your body, soul, and spirit. Take a moment to reflect on all the good things God has done for you and express your gratitude. The fact that you are alive, the fact that you are reading this book, is reason enough to open your mouth and thank Him. As you give thanks, I pray that your gratitude will activate the supernatural manifestation of God's glory in your life.

90

"For I received from the Lord that which I also delivered to you: that the Lord Jesus on the same night in which He was betrayed took bread; and when He had given thanks, He broke it and said, "Take, eat; this is My body which is broken for you; do this in remembrance of Me."" (1 Corinthians 11:23-24, NKJV).

Take the bread, break it, and say, "Father, as I take this bread, I thank you that Your body will supercharge my body with health and vitality."

"In the same manner He also took the cup after supper, saying, "This cup is the new covenant in My blood. This do, as often as you drink it, in remembrance of Me." For as often as you eat this bread and drink this cup, you proclaim the Lord's death till He comes." (1 Corinthians 11:25-26, NKJV).

"Lord, I thank you for your precious blood, which knew no sin. I thank you for redeeming me through your blood and for the better things it speaks over me. I am covered by Your precious blood. As I partake of your precious blood, let it bring life and health to my body. Thank you, Father, for the victorious power of Jesus' blood that knew no sin. I bless Your mighty name. Merciful Father, pour out Your mercies upon me. May my body manifest the benefits of communion. Renew my entire being! Restore health to my body and soul. You are the greatest Physician. Heal me, and I shall be healed. In Jesus' mighty name, Amen!"

Partake of His blood and give God thanks!

Concluding Prayer:

"O Lord, I thank You for all You have done for me. I give You all the praise and glory. Thank You for the grace You have released over my life to accomplish this. I am grateful for granting me the grace to seek Your face regarding my health and well-being."

"Precious Holy Spirit, grant me the grace and revelation to make this a lifestyle. As I dedicate this time to the restoration of my health, Lord, I ask for Your blessings to extend to my wealth, spiritual growth, and development. Shower me with blessings from every direction, O Lord! I give thanks to the Father, Son, and the precious Holy Spirit. May the face of the Lord shine upon me and may His glory rest upon me. In this season, I claim a double portion of His glory. In Jesus' mighty name, I pray. Amen!"

PHYSICAL

Food: I recommend fasting from 6 am to 6 pm and breaking the fast with Daniel Fast meals. If you are taking medication, I suggest adhering to Daniel Fast for breakfast, lunch, and dinner. Refer to the section "Foods to Enjoy" for suggestions.

Drink: Water is recommended. Aim to drink an average of 8-12 cups a day (2 – 3 liters). Healthy, caffeine-free herbal teas or raw vegetable juice are also good choices.

Exercise: "This is the day the Lord has made; We will rejoice and be glad in it." (Psalm 118:24, NKJV).

As today is the day the Lord has made, let us leap for joy by engaging in physical exercise. Commit to a minimum of 36.5 minutes of exercise, symbolizing 365 days in a year. You can choose activities like walking, dancing, running, jogging, swimming, biking, and more. Avoid remaining seated like idle individuals; instead, actively engage your

92

body. Move around and participate in some form of exercise.

"Physical exercise has some value, but spiritual exercise is valuable in every way, because it promises life both for the present and for the future." (1 Timothy 4:8, GNT).

As you engage in this exercise, meditate on the Word of God.

Conclusion

Congratulations on completing the Ten-Day Health Challenge, Daniel Fast, and Morning Battle Prayer. I know that the journey wasn't easy, but you did it! Take a moment to thank God for the grace that helped you finish strong. I encourage you to continue to incorporate the good habits you have developed into your day-to-day life. Let this become your new lifestyle.

You can integrate this practice monthly, once a quarter, or annually, depending on your conviction. Whatever you decide, I pray that the hand of God will be upon you, granting you divine health as your portion. May the abundant life promised by Jesus Christ become your reality. **"I came that they may have life, and have it in abundance [to the full, till it overflows]."** (John 10:10b, AMP).

The Assurance That You Are Going to Heaven

As I conclude this book, I would like to give the reader the opportunity to have the assurance that if they were to die today, they would make it to Heaven and be with Jesus.

The process is very simple and straightforward. First, repent of your sins for **"all have sinned and fall short of the glory of God"** (Romans 3:23, NKJV) and **"the wages of sin is death, but the gift of God is eternal life in Christ Jesus our Lord."** (Romans 6:23, NKJV). Next, believe in Jesus Christ, by faith, acknowledging that He came and died for your sins, that He is the gift of God. And finally, receive the gift, obey His Word, and follow Him.

94

"But as many as received Him, to them He gave the right to become children of God, to those who believe in His name" (John 1:12, NKJV).

If you would like to receive the gift that God has for you today, say this prayer and believe it in your heart.

"Dear Lord Jesus, I know that I am a sinner, and I cannot save myself through good works. Forgive me of my sins. Wash and cleanse me with the precious blood of Jesus. I believe you died for me. I believe you rose again. Today, I ask you to come into my heart and be my Lord and Savior. Thank you for accepting me as your child and giving me a new life. In Jesus' name. Amen!"

I would like to be the first to welcome you to the family of God. You are now born again. You are a child of God, and you will make it to Heaven!

Final Prayer

You are blessed! May the Face of God shine upon you, granting you divine health. May you experience immeasurable favor and may His glory rest upon you. You will never lack any good thing. Goodness and mercy will follow you. You are untouchable, immovable, and incorruptible; immortality shall be your portion, and the joy of the Lord will flood your life. You will testify and grow from faith to faith, from grace to grace, and from glory to glory. In Jesus' mighty and matchless name. Amen!

About The Author

Dr. George Ehigiator is a husband, father, pastor, evangelist, revivalist, motivational speaker, entrepreneur, and product developer. Born in Nigeria, Africa, he later moved to the United States of America. God is using him to accomplish tremendous works for His kingdom. With a calling to the ministry at a young age, he is advancing God's Kingdom on a global scale.

Dr. George Ehigiator is a genuine evangelist and revivalist known for moving in signs, wonders, and miracles. The anointing of the Lord upon him enables him to reach the unreachable and touch the untouchable with a message of hope, deliverance, and restoration. A passionate soul winner, he is committed to making it challenging for souls to go to hell. God uses him as a channel to demonstrate His love and power.

He holds a Bachelor's degree in Business Information Systems and a Master's degree in Business Administration. Additionally, Dr. George Ehigiator holds a Master's and a Doctorate degree in Divinity.

George and his lovely wife, Summer, are the Senior Pastors of NationTakers Ministries, a thriving church located in San Francisco, California. They were married in 2004, and God has blessed them with five amazing children.

To learn more about Dr. George Ehigiator and NationTakers Ministries, kindly follow us on all our social media platforms.

Pastor George Ehigiator

X: www.twitter.com/PastorGeorgee
Instagram: www.instagram.com/pastor_george_ehigiator
Facebook: www.facebook.com/drgeorgeehigiator
Website: www.GeorgeEhigiator.com

NationTakers Ministries

X: www.twitter.com/NationTakers
Instagram: www.instagram.com/nationtakers
Facebook: www.facebook.com/nationtakers
Website: www.NationTakers.com

Contact Author

Pastor George Ehigiator

NationTakers Ministries

info@nationtakers.com

nationtakers@gmail.com

(415) 337-7027

To access more resources on the Ten-Day Health Challenge, Daniel Fast, and Morning Battle, or to share your testimonies, visit www.GeorgeEhigiator.com.

About The Book

Ten-Day Health Challenge, Daniel Fast, & Morning Battle Prayer!

Are you experiencing health issues? Navigating a challenging season in life? Feeling stuck with no progress? This "Ten-Day Health Challenge, Daniel Fast, & Morning Battle Prayer" book will be your guide for a practical journey, spiritually and physically, leading you to achieve victory in challenging circumstances.

This book is designed for anyone aspiring to live a longer and healthier life, regardless of their struggles. By committing to this ten-day health challenge, Pastor George will guide you through a transformative process, enabling a complete makeover of your spirit, soul, and body. The outcome? Restoration of health, healing from sickness and disease, and the return of your joy and peace to your life.

Made in the USA
Las Vegas, NV
28 December 2023

83663462R00056